TES AIR FORCE

B-29
SUPERFORTRESS

Series Editor : Christopher Chant

Foulis

Haynes

Titles in the *Super Profile* series:

Boeing 707

B-29 Superfortress

Harrier

Further titles in this series will be published at
regular intervals. For information on new titles
please contact your bookseller or write to the
publisher.

ISBN 0 85429 339 6

A **FOULIS** Aircraft Book

First published 1983

© **1983 Winchmore Publishing Services Limited**

Published by:
Haynes Publishing Group
Sparkford,
Yeovil,
Somerset BA22 7JJ

Distributed in North America by:
Haynes Publications Inc.
861 Lawrence Drive,
Newbury Park,
California 91320, USA

Produced by:
Winchmore Publishing Services Limited,
40 Triton Square,
London NW1 3HG

Edited by Catherine Bradley
Designed by Andrzej Bielecki
Picture research Jonathan Moore
Printed in Hong Kong by Lee Fung Asco Limited.

Contents

Left: Sleek and powerful, the Boeing B-29 Superfortress was one of World War II's most important aircraft types.

4

A magnificent technical achievement developed in a relatively short period, the Boeing Model 345 strategic bomber entered service with the US Army Air Forces (USAAF) in 1943 as the B-29 Superfortress. It was a successor more than worthy of the admiration lavished on its predecessor, the B-17 Flying Fortress, and may justly be regarded as the world's first truly strategic aerial platform. There were many 'bugs' to be eliminated before the aircraft became an effective warplane, and then a number of tactical problems had to be overcome before the Superfortress could begin its task of burning the urban and industrial heart out of Japan in late 1944. As a result of the B-29s' efforts Japan had virtually no war-making potential left by mid-1945, but that determined nation refused to abandon the struggle until B-29s dropped the world's first (and so far only) operationally deployed nuclear weapons against the cities of Hiroshima and Nagasaki on 6 and 9 August 1945 respectively. It is for this horrendous episode that the Superfortress is best remembered, but the type went on to a fruitful career in the late 1940s and early 1950s.

Left: Even if Boeing had produced no other aircraft of note, the classic pair represented by the B-17 Flying Fortress and the B-29 Superfortress would have assured the company's fame. Seen here are an example of each type operated by the Confederate Air Force, based on Rebel Field at Harlingen, Texas. Though a linear descendant of the design philosophy that had produced the B-17, the B-29 appeared seven years later and was a markedly superior military machine reflecting the forced pace of aircraft development in the dire days leading up to World War II.

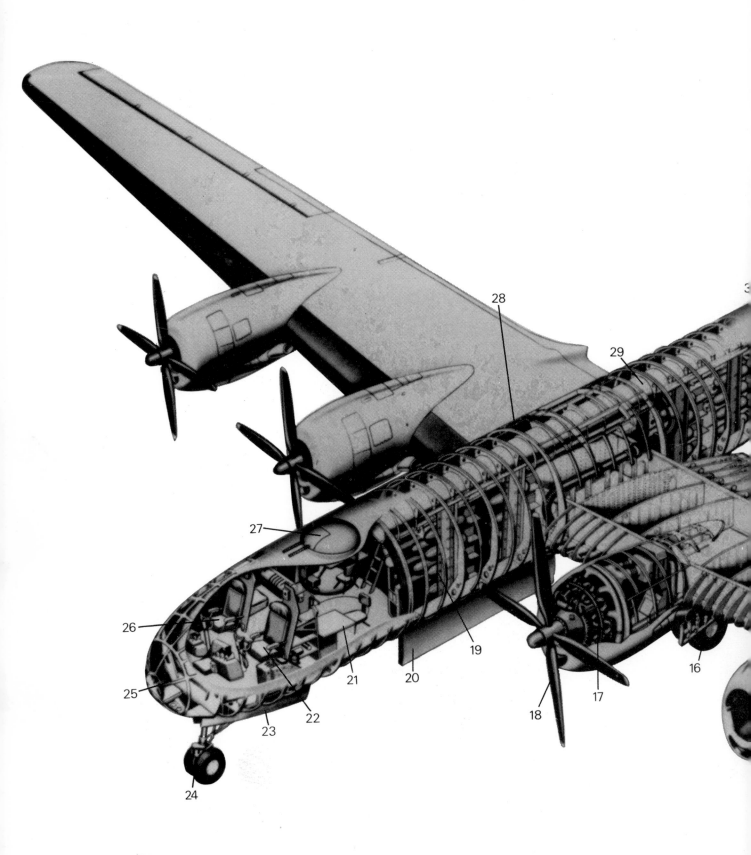

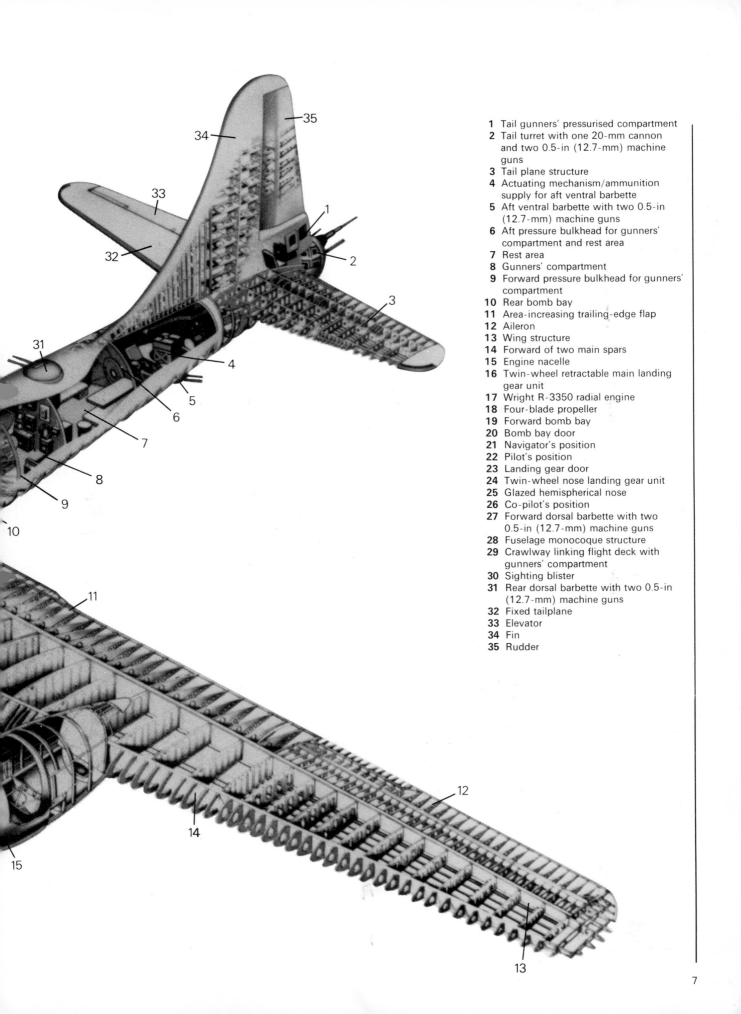

1 Tail gunners' pressurised compartment
2 Tail turret with one 20-mm cannon and two 0.5-in (12.7-mm) machine guns
3 Tail plane structure
4 Actuating mechanism/ammunition supply for aft ventral barbette
5 Aft ventral barbette with two 0.5-in (12.7-mm) machine guns
6 Aft pressure bulkhead for gunners' compartment and rest area
7 Rest area
8 Gunners' compartment
9 Forward pressure bulkhead for gunners' compartment
10 Rear bomb bay
11 Area-increasing trailing-edge flap
12 Aileron
13 Wing structure
14 Forward of two main spars
15 Engine nacelle
16 Twin-wheel retractable main landing gear unit
17 Wright R-3350 radial engine
18 Four-blade propeller
19 Forward bomb bay
20 Bomb bay door
21 Navigator's position
22 Pilot's position
23 Landing gear door
24 Twin-wheel nose landing gear unit
25 Glazed hemispherical nose
26 Co-pilot's position
27 Forward dorsal barbette with two 0.5-in (12.7-mm) machine guns
28 Fuselage monocoque structure
29 Crawlway linking flight deck with gunners' compartment
30 Sighting blister
31 Rear dorsal barbette with two 0.5-in (12.7-mm) machine guns
32 Fixed tailplane
33 Elevator
34 Fin
35 Rudder

Genesis

Boeing had long been associated with long-range heavy bombers even before the Model 299 was accepted for service by the US Army Air Corps (USAAC) and the successive USAAF as the B-17 series. Official US interest in long-range aerial bombardment had been something of a political pigeon ever since the traumatic period in the mid-1920s of General William 'Billy' Mitchell's court martial for prejudicing the relationship of the US Army and US Navy with his over-enthusiastic advocacy of the heavy bomber. There remained an inter-service rivalry as to which should operate such weapons, but on 14 April 1934 the USAAC issued a requirement for a 'Long Range Airplane Suitable for Military Purposes': this requirement was the result of tactical assessments conducted at Wright Field in 1933, postulating the landing of hostile forces in the remotest US territories, Alaska and the Hawaiian Islands. What the USAAC needed, therefore, was a bomber with a range in the order of 5,000 miles (8,047 km) so as to be able to operate against such forces and their support fleets from bases within the continental USA. Boeing and Martin each produced designs to the specification, and in July 1935 Boeing was awarded a development contract for one aircraft, designated Model 294 in Boeing's designation system, and XBLR-1 (for Experimental Bomber, Long Range-1) in the USAAC's terminology. This latter was altered to XB-15 (Experimental Bomber-15) in July 1936.

The XB-15 first flew on 15 October 1937, and was at that time the largest and heaviest aircraft yet built in the USA. As might be expected, the design incorporated a number of radical

features, many of which were to become standard on later aircraft. As might also be expected, so advanced an aircraft, at a time of rapid technological advance, was also obsolete in a number of other respects by the time of its first flight. Advanced features of this cantilever mid-wing monoplane, which was based on the Boeing design philosophy pioneered with the Model 200 Monomail of 1930, were considerable aerodynamic cleanliness; 110-volt AC power provided by generators driven by two auxiliary piston engines; galley and rest facilities for the crew on long missions; and a separate flightdeck station for the flight engineer, who thus eased the workload of the pilots by taking over the management of the four-engine powerplant. Retrograde features were a lack of turreted defensive armament, fabric covering for the wings aft of the main spar, and a wholly inadequate powerplant. The Boeing designers had originally planned for a quartet of Allison V-1710 inlines, but were then persuaded to adopt four 1,000-hp (746-kW) Pratt & Whitney R-1830 radials. Even with the Allisons the XB-15 would have been underpowered at a probable maximum take-off weight of about 70,750 lb chord ratio, and that even the provision of extra power would not significantly improve speed.

The eventual failure of the sole XB-15 should not be construed as a total loss for Boeing and the USA, for the Model 294 fixed in the designers' minds the concept of four-engine bombardment platforms, possessing great basic range and able to carry substantial bombloads over long distances. The Model 294 was conceived as a tactical bomber, however, and so too was its successor, the Model 299/B-17. Even though the Flying Fortress had four engines and was eventually used as a strategic weapon in the European theatre during World War II, it was conceived in response to a USAAC requirement of May 1934 for a multi-engine (by which the issuing authority implied two-engine) medium-range bomber able to carry a bombload of at least 2,000 lb (907 kg) over a radius of at least 1,020 miles (1,641 km) and preferably 2,200 miles (3,540 km) at a speed of not less than 200 mph (322 km/h) and hopefully of 250 mph (402 km/h). The Model 299 was considerably smaller than the Model 294, but of more advanced concept as it was based on Boeing's 'second-generation' of metal cantilever monoplanes, epitomised by the Model 247 airliner. Initially unsuccessful in production terms because of the USAAC's lack of financial resources at a time of entrenched US isolationism, the B-17 proved itself by a number of record-breaking flights and some spectacular feats in exercises. An already half-convinced USAAC finally decided that large-scale production should be instituted as rapidly as possible in the light of a deteriorating world situation. The faith shown in the B-17 by the USAAC and by the manufacturer was amply vindicated by the type's ubiquity and great success in World War II.

The family likeness of the B-17 and B-29 (background and foreground respectively) is evident in several ways, especially the tail unit. But the B-29 has a much more purposeful look to it with its cleaner lines, larger size and defensive armament located in barbettes.

(32,092 kg). As it was, the XB-15 weighed in at a maximum of 70,706 lb (32,072 kg) and, with a wing area of 2,780 sq ft (258.26 m²) and total power of 3,400 hp (2,536 kW) at 5,000 ft (1,525 m), had a maximum speed of only 200 mph (322 km/h) and the poor service ceiling of 18,900 ft (5,760 m). Maximum offensive load was a useful 8,000 lb (3,629 kg) and

defensive armament, though inadequately mounted, was relatively heavy at two 0.5-in (12.7-mm) and four 0.3-in (7.62-mm) machine-guns. The two factors that really defeated the XB-15 as the basis for strategic bomber development were lack of power and the rapidly accelerating pace of technical developments in the middle and late 1930s. The provision of the advanced features already mentioned, plus others such as split flaps and twin-wheel main landing gear units, could not alter the fact that the design was based on a very large wing of considerable thickness/

136954

A Patient Evolution

By 1938 the USAAC had gained sufficient experience with the first examples of the Y1B-17A (Model 299F) service test aircraft to be able to gauge how the next generation of heavy bombers should be developed. The service had insufficient financial resources to fund the construction of any prototype, so Boeing had to be content to proceed with a series of design studies reflecting the USAAC's requirements but sponsored financially by the company in the hope of future orders.

The USAAC's first thoughts towards an improved B-17 resulted in the **Model 334** design, which incorporated cabin pressurisation and a tricycle landing gear arrangement for better crew performance at high altitude and for better runway performance respectively. In July 1939 this design, which had already evolved through interim stages designated **Models 316**, **322** and **333** by Boeing, became the **Model 334A**. This may be regarded as the immediate predecessor of the Superfortress and, still at its own expense, the company built a detailed mock-up of the improved **Model 341** in December 1939.

Boeing was thus well placed when, on 29 January 1940, the War Department responded to a request by Major General H. H. Arnold (Chief of the Air Corps) for a 'superbomber' by issuing Requirement 40B. This called for a bomber capable of 400 mph (644 km/h) and able to deliver a bombload of 2,000 lb (907 kg) over a radius of 2,665 miles (4,289 km). But no sooner had the specification been issued than it was amended in the light of information beginning to arrive from Europe about the nature of combat air operations in that continent: greater protection was required, and

improved gun armament, additional armour and the provision of self-sealing tanks were demanded. In this revised form the specification issued on 5 February 1940 called for a 'Hemisphere Defense Weapon' with a maximum bombload of 16,000 lb (7,258 kg).

The Boeing Model 341 design (2,000 lb/907 kg bombload carried over 7,000 miles/ 11,265 km at 405 mph/652 km/h) could not meet the exacting requirements of this specification, and was thus refined further into the definitive **Model 345** which met all the USAAC's demands except that for speed, which was estimated at 382 mph (615 km/h). Boeing's final proposal

was submitted to the USAAC on 11 May 1940. Other submissions were received from Consolidated, Douglas and Lockheed, and the USAAC had a hard time deciding an initial order of merit between the designs of these four giants of the American aviation industry. By 27 June 1940 the USAAC had reached its decision, and announced that further engineering data were being funded for the designs now identified, in order of merit from the top, as the **Boeing XB-29**, Lockheed XB-30, Douglas XB-31 and Consolidated XB-32. Douglas and Lockheed pulled out of the competition without too much delay, leaving the field to Boeing and Consolidated.

Right from the start, the B-29 was conceived round a powerplant comprising four turbocharged radial engines. There was a single inline-engined variant in the form of the XB-39, a conversion engineered by General Motors to evaluate the possibility of such an arrangement.

Further progress was rapid, and on 24 August 1940 money was appropriated for prototype construction, the USAAC signing for two flight and one static test articles on 6 September. The contract was revised in December 1940 to provide for a third flight prototype. Boeing had meanwhile been finalising the design of the Model 345, and in May 1941 the contracting authorities were able to inspect a new mockup of the proposed aircraft.

During the same month the US Army told Boeing that it intended to order 250 production B-29s, to be built at the new Plant 2, a government-owned production facility, at Boeing Wichita. (On 8 April 1939 Stearman Aircraft Company, a wholly owned Boeing subsidiary, had become the Wichita Division of the parent Boeing Airplane Company, with production capability rapidly expanded to meet the anticipated growth in the services' orders for the trainers in whose design Stearman excelled.) Construction of the first prototype, the XB-29 serialled 41-002, had been begun even before the final inspection of the mock-up, and in September 1941 the USAAF (as the USAAC had become on 20 June 1941 with the issuing of Army Regulation 95-5) placed its first contract for 250 B-29s, increased to 500 production examples in January 1942 after the USA had been pulled into World War II. The scale of eventual production now envisaged by the USAAF is indicated by the company's receipt in February 1942 of instructions to prepare the way for co-production of the B-29 by Bell Aircraft Corporation at Marietta, Georgia, by North American Aviation Inc at Kansas City, Kansas, and by the Fisher Body Division of the General Motors Corporation at Cleveland, Ohio. The planned production programme also showed how badly the USAAF needed the new bomber, Pearl Harbor and the USA's consequent entry into World War II having found the USAAF well prepared in basic planning (with that most important aspect of air force growth, a well expanded training base of aircraft and men, fully under way) but poorly placed in the development of adequate combat aircraft, though several great types were in small-scale service or the last stages of development.

It is interesting to note that the only comparable production programme for an aircraft which had not yet flown was that for the Martin B-26 Marauder, of which the USAAC had ordered 201 'off the drawing board' in 1939. Even so, the Marauder was a smaller and less complex aircraft than the B-29, with two rather than four engines, so the magnitude of the B-29 programme was perhaps 10 or more times greater.

Below: A torrent of B-29s, one of the four major production lines for the series.
Right: A completed B-29 is towed out onto the test apron during 1944. The next step was flight trials.

Boeing XB-29

Apart from the administrative and financial problems associated with the diversification and sub-contracting effort for B-29 production, Boeing's principal concern at Seattle was the completion of the XB-29 first prototype, which was being completed without armament in an effort to speed development of the airframe/powerplant combination. Even so, the XB-29 was so ambitious a project that problems were continually encountered, and the Boeing designers showed enormous skill and ingenuity in overcoming these. As they were trying to come to grips with these basic problems, their troubles were compounded by the inevitable stream of demands from the USAAF for greater operational performance, especially in terms of bombload, speed, range and defensive firepower. The steady increase in maximum take-off weight entailed by these demands pushed wing loading higher and, mindful of the similar problems faced by the Marauder, the USAAF pressed Boeing for an increase in wing area to reduce wing loading. Boeing was loath to do this: the programme would be considerably delayed by any decision to evolve a wing of greater area and, at the same time, greater area would require a restressed wing of higher structure weight and more drag, with consequent degradation of the aircraft's performance, whose steady improvement was constantly demanded by USAAF planners and technical staffs. The USAAF's fears about wing loading were well-founded, for what was envisaged was a machine with a maximum loading of about 60 lb/sq ft (293 kg/m^2), com-

pared with the 53 lb/sq ft (259 kg/m²) for the B-26 already suffering a high loss rate in training as a result of pilots' inexperience with such a highly loaded aircraft. But Boeing had a partial solution to the problem in the form of Fowler-type trailing-edge flaps: these not only increased lift coefficient when deployed, but also increased wing area by about 20 per cent, thus reducing the wing loading at take-off to about 50.4 lb/sq ft (245.8 kg/m²). The use of tricycle landing gear on the B-26 had also proved of great value to pilots during high-speed take-off

and landing runs, and such a landing gear configuration had been selected for the B-29 series in preference to the tailwheel type used by the B-17 and most other heavy military aircraft of the day. To validate the basic designs of the B-29 series' flying surfaces, scaled-down equivalents were test flown with complete success on a modified Fairchild PT-19A trainer.

The XB-29 had no defensive armament, and was intended primarily for evaluation of the airframe/powerplant combination. It is seen here with its two port engines being run up during a trial. The four propellers were each three-blade units.

Apart from the difficulties of compressing so much aircraft into so small a volume in relative terms, the two other areas in which the Boeing design team faced most problems were pressurisation and defensive armament. The B-29 was intended to operate at altitudes in excess of 30,000 ft (9,145 m), so pressurised accommodation for the crew was essential. Boeing had experience with pressurisation, which was still a novelty in the late 1930s, with the Model 307 Stratoliner, and this experience was of great help to the designers. However, the

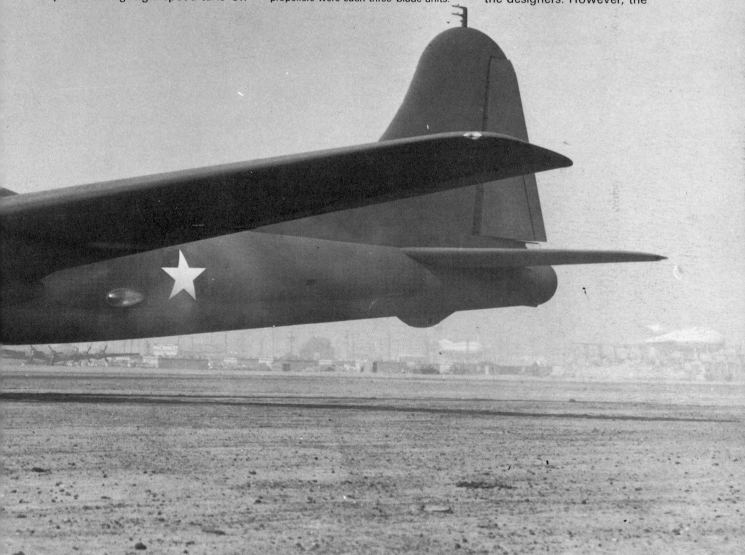

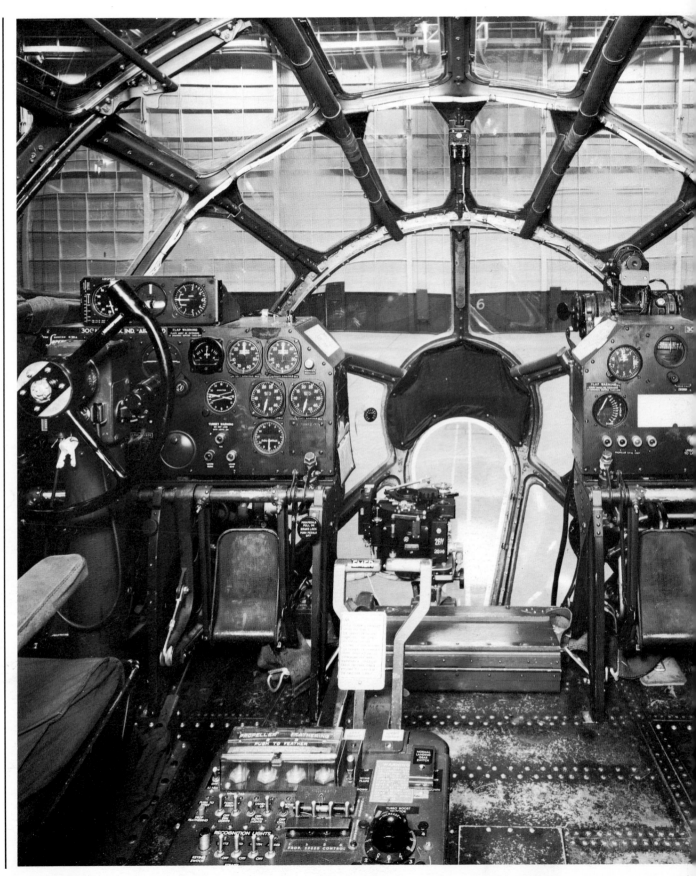

The pilot (left) and co-pilot (right) had excellent fields of vision, and so too did the bombardier, seated centrally below and in front of the pilots.

Stratoliner had been designed as a civil aircraft with an operating ceiling of about 20,000 ft (6,095 m). In the pressurisation system for the B-29 the designers had to consider the exigencies of military operations and the concomitant possibility of combat damage, as well as the need of the B-29 to operate at least 50 per cent higher than the Model 307, which may be regarded as the pressurised civil transport version of the Model 299 (B-17 series). Structural problems with the sealing of so large a fuselage combined with fears of system failure as a result of combat damage to persuade the designers of the B-29 to adopt only partial pressurisation, concentrated on the main crew stations.

Thus the nose section, with its extensively glazed hemispherical front, was pressurised to provide comfortable working conditions for the flightdeck crew, consisting of the command pilot, co-pilot, flight engineer, navigator, radio operator and bombardier. Aft of the wing, and connected with the forward section by a pressurised tunnel, was a second pressurised compartment, this time for the central gunnery controller, and left and right gunners. Finally, the rear defence of the aircraft was entrusted to a rear gunner who inhabited a third, and entirely independent, pressurised compartment in the extreme tail. This last compartment could be entered and left only when there was no pressurisation of the system.

The engine selected for the Superfortress was the totally new Wright R-3350 twin-row air-cooled radial, rated at some 2,200 hp (1,641 kW) and set in four nacelles cantilevered from the forward portion of the inner wing panels. The most important

aspect of the powerplant, however, was the need to keep power output as high as possible up to the greatest possible altitude, for only thus could the B-29 attain the range and over-target performance that would provide a measure of immunity from both fighter and anti-aircraft artillery opposition. The Superfortress was planned, therefore, with two turbochargers to each engine, the turbochargers for each nacelle being located aft of the oiler coolers and turbocharger intercooler placed at the bottom of the oval (with the long axis vertical) nacelles. To ensure optimum propeller efficiency in the upper atmosphere, relatively low propeller revolutions were necessary, and to this end the R-3350s were provided with gearing to produce an output of 35 revolutions to each 100 put in by the engine crankshaft.

Construction of the three prototypes was pushed ahead at all speed in the Boeing Plant 1 at Seattle, and then moved by road to Boeing Field for assembly and flight tests. All was ready for the historic take-off in September 1942, by which time production contracts for more than 1,650 Superfortresses had been placed. On 21 September Boeing's chief test pilot, Edward 'Eddie' Allen, lifted 41-002 into the air for the type's maiden flight. Power was provided by four R-3350-13 radials driving three-blade propellers, and the aircraft handled well.

There was little radical about the aircraft, which was an exceptionally clean mid-wing cantilever monoplane of metal construction (apart from fabric-covered control surfaces) with low-drag nacelles and retractable tricycle landing gear with twin wheels on each unit. Where the XB-29 was different from contemporary heavy bombers was in its specification (particularly those aspects dealing with range and speed) and the fact that it combined so many 'state of the art' features in one airframe. Perhaps the most radical feature was the defensive armament, but this was not fitted to the first prototype as noted above. The second XB-29 (41-003) followed the first into the air on 28 December 1942, but was lost while Eddie Allen was trying to land it with a raging engine fire at Boeing Field on 18 February 1943. Together with Allen, 10 other valuable flight test crew were lost in this disaster, which presaged many similar engine fires that were to plague the service life of the B-29.

The third XB-29 (41-18335) was assembled at Wichita, where a service-test batch of 14 **YB-29** aircraft was under construction in the government-built facility run by Boeing. The third XB-29 incorporated many of the detail improvements found desirable as a result of the flight trials of the first and second prototypes, and took to the air for the first time in June 1943, which month also saw the first YB-29 in the air, on 26 June. By the end of July seven YB-29s had been completed, allowing an intensification of the arduous test programme.

The original defensive armament fit consisted of a tail position with two 0.5-in (12.7-mm) Browning M2 machine-guns and one 20-mm M2 Type B cannon, plus four retractable fuselage turrets of Sperry manufacture, each fitted with a pair of 0.5-in (12.7-mm) M2 guns and controlled by gunners using periscopic sights. This fit was installed in the ill-fated second XB-29, and while the retractable turrets were a modest boon to performance when retracted, they added considerably to the system's complexity and hence to lack of reliability. The definitive defensive armament fit was thus a General Electric system, fitted to the third XB-29 and immediately proved superior. The same turret disposition was

The third XB-29 is seen in flight over typical 'Boeing country' in the state of Washington. This aircraft pioneered the General Electric turret/blister system.

retained, with a remotely controlled tail position supplemented by twin-gun units in forward and aft dorsal and ventral locations; but the control and sighting arrangement was altered, a tactical gunnery controller supervising the efforts of three gunners (tail, upper and lower). The pair of dorsal turrets was controlled by the upper gunner, who sat in a 'barber chair' under a small dome (offering 360° field of vision over the whole upper hemisphere) made of three bonded layers of Plexiglass, and

Boeing Wichita got into the Superfortress programme with the YP-29 service-test model. This was the seventh of 14 such aircraft, all finished in olive-drab.

located in the top of the tactical compartment aft of the wing. The gunner was provided with a sight that computed deflection and parallax factors automatically, and a similar sight was used by the lower gunner who controlled the two ventral turrets from the pair of domes on the fuselage sides in the tactical compartment. The tail position could be fired from the waist positions in an emergency, and the bombardier could assume control of the forward ventral and dorsal positions as required. The four fuselage turrets had ammunition stowage amounting to 1,000 rounds per gun, and the whole system though conceptually complex proved highly effective.

Boeing YB-29

The 14 YB-29 service-test aircraft were externally identical with the third XB-29 but were powered by the R-3350-21 radial, though the three-blade propeller of the XB-29s was retained. This had a diameter of 17 ft (5.18 m), and was later replaced on production aircraft by a four-blade Hamilton Standard propeller with a diameter of 16 ft 7 in (5.05 m). All the YB-29 aircraft were finished in standard USAAF camouflage, and were used for a rapidly increased trials and operational evaluation programme.

This was concerned with all aspects of the Superfortress bomber project, but concentrated on proving the entire bomber as a combat weapon, and testing the armament installation. This was particularly important for the offensive armament, which had not been evaluated fully with the XB-29s. Bomb stowage was provided in two bays, located in front of and behind the wing main spar structure. (This, it should be noted, was perhaps Boeing's most radical departure from its standard construction philosophy, for the conventional bridge-type truss was replaced in the B-29 by a web-type construction for the wings.) The placing of the two bays relatively far forward and aft of the centre of gravity meant that a special bomb-drop system had to be used, with an intervalometer used to ensure that bombs were dropped alternately from the bays to maintain the centre of gravity in the right position. Loads tested and approved for the B-29 production version were four 4,000-lb (1,814-kg), or eight 2,000-lb (907-kg), or 12 1,000-lb (454-kg), or 40 500-lb (227-kg), or 50 300-lb (136-kg) or 80 100-lb (45-kg) bombs. All these loads could be carried without modification to the bomb bays, though it is worth noting that by the end of World War II, B-29s were fitted to carry a more diverse load, comprising incendiaries or a mixture of incendiary and HE bombs, and that some aircraft had been modified to single-bay configuration for the carriage of a single 44,000-lb (19,958-kg) weapon. Other B-29s were adapted to carry two large 'blockbuster' bombs on special racks fitted under the wings between the fuselage and the inboard engine nacelles. Subsequent evolution of the B-29 series' 'bomb bay' resulted in the aircraft's ability to uplift a variety of research aircraft, which could then be air-launched in the USA's ambitious evolution of supersonic aircraft.

The first YB-29 is three-point weighed.

Serial number 42-24579 was the B-29-40-BW *Eddie Allen* of the 45th Bomb Squadron, 40th Bomb Group, US 20th Air Force. The aircraft, one of the first to be deployed overseas, is seen with bomb and camel markings under the cockpit, denoting bombing and transport ('over the hump') missions respectively.

Boeing B-29

Even before the initial delivery of YB-29 service-test aircraft, the first USAAF Superfortress unit was formed, the 58th (Very Heavy) Bombardment Wing coming into existence on 1 June 1943 as part of a programme of development and training which, the USAAF realised, would have to be pursued with considerable vigour and flexibility if the **B-29** was to get into combat without too inordinate a delay. As is

always the case with prototypes, the XB-29s and YB-29s were superior aircraft to initial production aircraft, for they were almost hand-built by highly skilled personnel reserved for such tasks. The initial teething problems of production aircraft from Boeing alone would have been difficult enough, but the hopes pinned on rapid production by Boeing and its associates meant that aircraft were moving along vast lines at a time when a host of problems had been appreciated but not solved. One of the most massive subcontract

programmes ever launched was associated with the Superfortress production plan, and major production centres were operational at Marietta (Bell) and Omaha, Nebraska (Glenn L. Martin Company). This latter had been brought in as a replacement for the Fisher Body Division, which was now producing major components as part of the scheme to boost the speed of Superfortress production. A fourth major production source was also being geared up for B-29 production. This was a Boeing-run facility at Renton, quite close to Seattle in

Left: Seen in pristine condition, 427334 (44-27334) *Noah's Ark* was a Martin-built B-29-MO of that plant's third (out of four) production batches. The nosewheel steering was considered heavy on the B-29, and the B-50 series introduced hydraulic steering to ease the problem.
Below: Built as a B-29-BW, 224528 (42-24528) was later revised to this YB-29J standard to test the revised 'Andy Gump' nacelles intended for late-production B-29A aircraft.
Right: The capacious bomb bays of the B-29 could carry a diverse load of free-fall weapons, and were later modified to permit the air-launch of research aircraft.
Below right: This claustrophobic crawlway was the only means of movement between the pressurised flightdeck and gunners' compartments.
Below far right: The pressurised nose compartments of B-29s under construction.

Washington state. The facility had been built by the US Navy for production of the Boeing PBB-1 Sea Ranger patrol flying-boat, which was terminated when it was realised that existing land-based aircraft such as the Consolidated B-24 Liberator could fulfil the same role without the need for new production. The Renton facility was then handed over to the US Army in exchange for the US Army-owned facility at Kansas City, which was run by North American Aviation.

By the early part of 1944, therefore, Superfortress bombers were starting to pour in from the Wichita Division of Boeing as **B-29-BW**, from Bell at Marietta as **B-29-BA** and from Martin at Omaha as **B-29-MO** aircraft. These were fitted with R-3350-23, -23A or -41 radials and cleared at maximum take-off weights ranging between 133,500 and 138,000 lb (60,556 and 62,597 kg).

The USAAF had a potential world-beater. But production-line aircraft built before the final ironing out of all the development snags could not be considered as combat-ready, and so the USAAF resorted to a remarkable expedient to raise existing aircraft to operational standards without disrupting the steady flow on the production lines. This expedient is generally known as the 'Battle of Kansas', a frantic period of some six weeks between 10 March and 15 April 1944. Special modification centres were established at air bases in Kansas and at the Omaha and Marietta production plants, with USAAF personnel supported by considerable numbers of Boeing workers. The problems were enormous: the

USAAF ground crews had little or no experience·with the B-29; spares and even tools were in desperately short supply; and, perhaps worst of all, virtual blizzard conditions hampered the working conditions of men operating in the open. Surprisingly enough, the removal of skilled men from Wichita and Seattle did not affect matters there too adversely, and by April 1944 the first B-29s were judged ready for overseas deployment, the training effort of the 58th (VH) Bombardment Wing having borne valuable fruit in the form of a trained USAAF nucleus from which would grow a decisive offensive weapon.

There had been considerable disagreement within the US high command as to the theatre to which the Superfortress should be deployed. In keeping with the USA's policy of 'Germany first', it was reasonably suggested that the type should be used to batter Germany into submission. But by the end of 1943 it had been decided that the B-29's range and payload suited the type better for the inauguration of a strategic bombardment campaign against Japan, which could not be attacked by other aircraft such as the B-17 and B-24 that were admirably suited to European operations. Thus was formed the 20th Air Force, intended specifically for the assault on Japan from bases in India and China, where the XX Bomber Command was located. In the utmost secrecy, therefore, the four groups of the 58th (VH) Bombardment wing (the 40th, 444th, 462nd and 468th Bombardment Groups) made their way via Africa to India.

B-29s of the 39th Bomb Group,
314th Bomb Wing, 20th Air Force (based
on Guam), unload their incendiaries over
Japan on 16 July 1945.

Superfortresses of the 500th
Bomb Group, 73rd Bomb Wing, 20th Air
Force, drop unwieldy but terribly efficient
fire bombs on Yokohama during a raid on
29 May 1945.

The Wright R-3350 radial was a mighty engine, its 3,350-cu in (54.9-litre) capacity turning out some 2,200 hp (1,641 kW) at 2,600 revolutions per minute. Maintenance of high power output up to extreme altitude was ensured by the provision of two turbochargers to each engine, the turbochargers' intercooler being fed with air through the small inlet at the base of the nacelle, which also fed the oil coolers.

Right: Clearly visible on this grounded B-29A are the four-gun forward dorsal turrets designed to deal with the Axis powers' favoured head-on fighter attacks; the twin bomb bays in front of and behind the aircraft's centre of gravity, this requiring the use of an intervalometer to ensure that bombs were released alternately from the forward and after bays; and the tail bumper to ensure that the undersurface of the rear fuselage did not scrape along the runway as the aircraft rotated at take-off.
Left: A trio of B-29s in flight. The natural metal finish was standard after Axis fighter defences declined, higher speed more than compensating for the polished metal's greater glare. The Superfortress nearest the camera is a B-29-BW, the 29th aircraft from a run of 200 that was Boeing Wichita's fourth (out of five) production batch.
Below: A highly-polished B-29A on the tarmac before the installation of its four-gun forward dorsal turret. The use of a four- rather than two-gun turret in this position increased forward-firing gunpower by 50 per cent, to six 0.5-in (12.7-mm) M2 Browning machine-guns.

Above: Seated on the left of the flight-deck, the pilot was also the captain of the Superfortress, and thus primarily responsible for the operation of the entire aircraft/crew combination as an effective combat unit.

Above left: The backbone of the USA's long-range bomber arm since World War II has been the Strategic Air Command, whose first major weapon system was the Superfortress.

Left: In common with the B-17, the B-29 proved a fertile bed for nose art, that peculiarly American form of military self-expression.

Below left: The sole Superfortress in the UK is a B-29A which was delivered by air to the Imperial War Museum, Duxford on 2 March 1980. The aircraft, much in need of renovation, is seen in the Korean War markings of the 307th Bomb Group, Strategic Air Command, with which it spent its operational career. The aircraft was delivered in May 1945 and saw no service in World War II, although 30 missions were flown in the Korean conflict. The aircraft was allocated to the Naval Ordnance Test Station (later Naval Weapons Center) at China Lake, and was prepared for the flight to the UK by Aero Services at the Pima Air Museum in Arizona.

Right: A nose view of the Superfortress reveals the hemispherically clean lines of the aircraft's 'sharp end', the multi-panel glazing, the optically-flat panel for the bombardier and the twin-wheel nose unit of the landing gear.

Inset right: The exhaust gases drove the turbochargers before exiting from the nacelle.

Above: With the engine instrumentation delegated to the flight engineer, only a small battery of primary flight instruments was needed for the co-pilot (illustrated) and pilot.

Above left: Much experimentation into an optimum defensive gun disposition was carried out with the Superfortress (including a manual nose gun and remotely-controlled cheek guns on the lower sides of the nose), but the originally conceived arrangement was ultimately retained. Seen here is one of the lateral waist gunners with his computing sight. These two gunners had primary control of the aft ventral barbette, with secondary control of the forward ventral barbette and tail guns. All the guns were fitted with electric interrupters to prevent them firing at any part of their own aircraft.

Left: The task of the flight engineer was complex, and amounted to the total control of the powerplant and its fuel system, with quadruple controls for the synchronisation of matters such as mixture, throttle and boost settings.

Right: The rear gunner in his separate tail compartment had primary control of one 20-mm M2 Type B cannon and two 0.5-in (12.7-mm) M2 machine-guns.

Right: Compared with the B-29, the B-50A was a much improved aircraft. Among the visible alterations were the taller tail, revised engine nacelles and the elegantly streamlined forward dorsal turret. Also notable are the 'buzz numbers' on the fuselage sides: these were introduced after World War II, BK indicating the B-50 basic type and the numbers being the last three digits of the serial number.

Below: The serial number 8052 (more fully 48-052) identifies this Superfortress as an example of the definitive B-50D series. The red stripe through the backing rectangle of the national marking was ordained in January 1947.

Right: B-29s of the 29th Bomb Group come under attack from a Kawasaki Ki-45 'Nick' heavy fighter. Such a threat was small, for even if the Japanese could get their fighters into the air in time to intercept, the indifferent quality of the pilots made attacks relatively harmless. Additionally, the 'Nick' was some 20 mph (32 km/h) slower than the Superfortress, making interception doubly difficult.
Below: There were losses, however, and here a B-29 heads back towards base with one engine on fire. Radio information from other B-29s, coupled with the presence over the sea of 'Dumbo' and 'Superdumbo' rescue aircraft, meant that the crews of Superfortresses which had to ditch generally faced few survival problems before being picked up by a rescue flying-boat.

With the 20th and 21st Air Forces

The crews of the first four groups in Asia were well acquainted with the B-29 by the time they began to arrive in India and China in April 1944, and thus needed only to familiarise themselves with the theatre before beginning operations. The only trouble lay in the nature of the bases in China, which had been prepared by the most stupendous manual efforts of some hundreds of thousands of Chinese peasants: though the runways were long and flat enough, and within range of the Japanese home islands, they were incredibly dusty in the dry season and seas of mud in the wet season. Moreover, maintenance facilities were non-existent, and supplies of fuel and ammunition very small. Thus for every B-29 deployed operationally to China, another two were employed ferrying fuel, bombs, machine-gun ammunition and even tools of the front-line bases. It was hardly the way to run an effective offensive campaign, but it was all that could be achieved at the time, and a very great achievement in its own right.

The first operational mission by the Superfortress was mounted from India, in the event, and its target was the capital of Thailand, Bangkok, which was attacked on 5 June 1944. The first raid on Japan followed 10 days later when Superfortresses from Chengtu raided the steel mills at Yawata, only 61 aircraft returning safely. However, of the seven B-29s lost, only one succumbed to enemy action. This was to set the pattern for further Superfortress operations from China, where bases in territory unoccupied by the Japanese were too far from Japan for effective missions. The outward journey was bad enough, with problems of weather and navigation to be

overcome, but the return trip was worse, with the same problems as the outward leg and also the worries of combat damage and fuel shortage. In these circumstances the attrition rate was high and results poor. The Japanese quickly recognised that this initial campaign boded ill for the future, and the B-29 bases were among the primary targets for the offensive launched in the middle of 1944 south of Changsha.

The turning point in the air campaign against Japan was the capture of the Marianas islands in the middle of 1944: two huge bases were built on Guam, a further two on Tinian and one on Saipan, able to accommodate some 900 aircraft between them. The round trip to Japan was still some 3,000 miles (4,825 km), but this was less than the trip faced by China-based aircraft, and better maintenance and support facilities were soon established in the Marianas. Moreover, the subsequent capture of Iwo Jima (about half way between the Marianas and Japan) provided an emergency landing spot for damaged bombers and a base for escort fighters which could thus operate with the bombers over Japan.

The engineering and logistic effort needed to ready the Marianas bases was enormous, but B-29s from China began to transfer to the new bases later in 1944. The first raid from the Marianas comprised 111 B-29s in a mission to the Musashino aero engine factory in Tokyo during 24 November 1944. But only 24 of the force actually attacked the primary target, and as usual the Americans found accurate bomb-aiming difficult if not impossible in the jetstream winds in which they were operating. Some indication of this

factor is given by the results achieved against the Musashino plant, which had received one-third of the total B-29 effort but had been only 4 per cent destroyed. It was clear that there was little wrong with the B-29 as a bomber, so the fault inevitably lay with the crews or with the tactics used. A new man was brought in to sort out the problem: Major General Curtis E. LeMay, lately controller of China-based B-29 operations, assumed command of XXI Bomber Command on 20 January 1945, and spent the first weeks of his new responsibility in assessing the situation with great dispassion. LeMay unleashed his thunderbolt on 9 March 1945: there would be a total reversal of B-29 tactics, with daylight high-altitude raids using HE bombs replaced by night raids at low and medium altitudes using incendiaries or a mixture of incendiaries and HE. LeMay correctly reasoned that the densely packed Japanese cities, with industrial areas cheek-by-jowl with residential areas, were the prime target: the incendiaries would destroy the largely wood-built accommodation of the Japanese industrial workforce, as well as causing widespread loss of life and damage to urban systems, while the HE would break up the concrete bases on which were supported the machine-tools used by Japan's war industries. With these latter smashed, it was relatively immaterial whether or not the machine-tools themselves had been destroyed.

Built very close to each other on the Boeing Wichita production line, a pair of 20th Air Force B-29 Superfortresses head across country. LeMay's amazing tactical revision of 1945 meant that all defensive armament other than the tail guns was removed in the Far Eastern theatre.

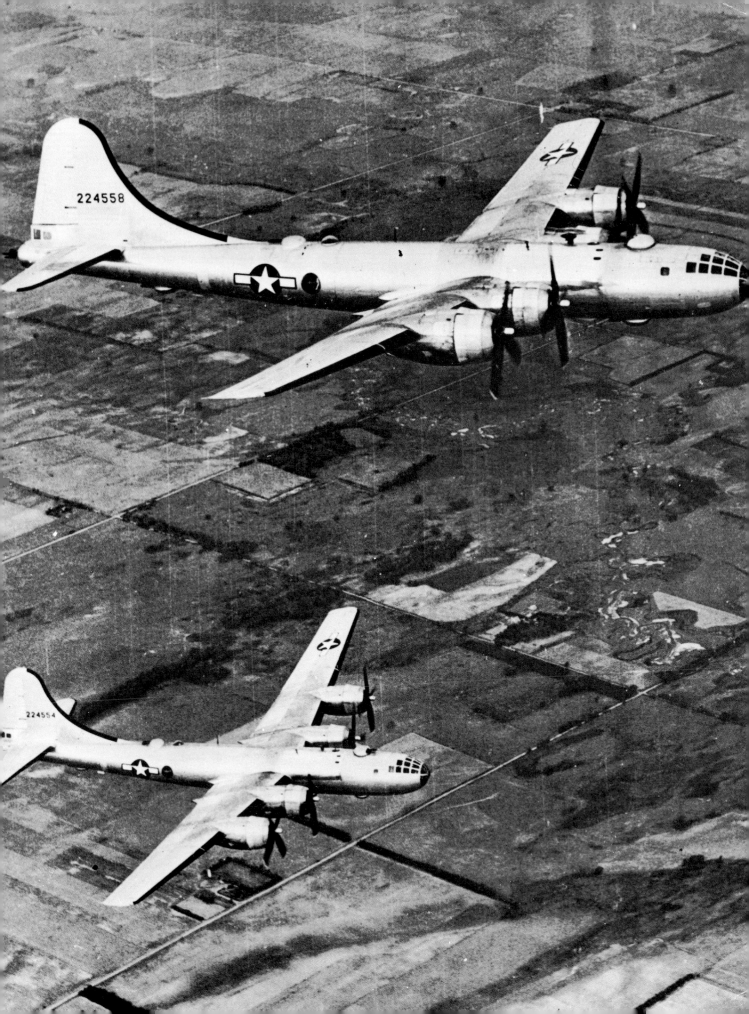

LeMay also announced that attacks would be individual, that altitude was to be between 5,000 and 8,000 ft (1,525 and 2,440 m) and that only tail armament was to be carried, as the Japanese had no effective night-fighter force and the weight thus saved could be used for greater offensive load. The net effect of LeMay's about-turn of American bomber tactics was vastly increased bombload delivered to the target, for a B-29 operating as a singleton at medium altitude could carry very nearly three times the payload of a B-29 in formation at high altitude. This meant that Japan could be attacked more accurately with bombloads comprising some 16,000 lb (7,258 kg) of M69 fire bombs per aircraft. Each M69 was a cluster of incendiaries round a core of petrol jelly, a thoroughly unpleasant but highly effective weapon combining the worst features of the incendiary and napalm bombs.

LeMay's decision left only two weeks of offensive operations against Japan before his forces were scheduled to co-operate with other US forces in the assault on Okinawa, the final stepping stone in the campaign to put American forces within invasion distance of the Japanese home islands. LeMay and his planners had four major targets (Tokyo, Nagoya, Osaka and Kobe) for destruction as strategic objectives, and decided to attack all four before the 23 March 1945 deadline. First on the list was Tokyo, and on the night of 9–10 March 334 Superfortresses were despatched against the city: losses were considered high at 14 aircraft, but the result was the single most devastating air attack of all time, with about 16.5 square miles of the city completely devastated by 1,667 tons of fire bombs. This area of devastation comprised about 85 per cent of the whole Tokyo target area, and among the places destroyed were

32 targets listed for pinpoint attack. Japanese casualties totalled about 200,000 dead and injured. The next target was Nagoya, raided on the night of 11–12 March with disappointing results (1.56 square miles destroyed). On 14–15 March it was the turn of Osaka, where 13,000 casualties were caused and 8.1 square miles destroyed by some 300 Superfortresses. Finally it was the turn of Kobe, where on the night of 16–17 March the

B-29s wiped out some 2.4 square miles of the city and caused about 15,000 casualties. LeMay even had time to spare for a return visit to Nagoya on 19 March, when some 300 aircraft dropped about 2,000 tons of fire bombs so closely that a firestorm of real size failed to develop, and only 0.65 square miles were gutted. This last raid was the reverse of that of the previous week, when the bombs had been too scattered for the creation of

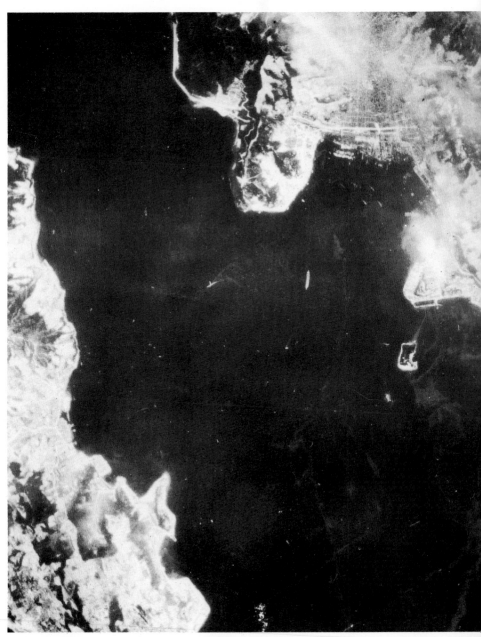

a firestorm. But for an overall loss rate of a mere 1.3 per cent, LeMay had in just 11 days burned the heart out of Japan: 29 square miles had been destroyed by 10,100 tons of bombs for an insignificant loss rate, and with the advent of fighter escorts from Iwo Jima from April, the pace of raids could be increased as the whole of Japan came under the threat of LeMay's torch. Losses continued to fall, and by August

1945 had reached a mere 0.02 per cent. However, on one occasion the crews of the Superfortresses met effective opposition: this was a raid against Tokyo on the night of 25–26 May 1945, when 464 of 498 B-29s despatched attacked the target to destroy an unexceeded 18.9 square miles (with few civilian losses as most of Tokyo's surviving population had left the city). Some 26 aircraft were lost to enemy action, and a further

100 were damaged by AA fire. Losses were thus 5.6 per cent, damaged aircraft 21.3 per cent, and aircrew losses were 254. Other than this, the incendiary-carrying B-29s could roam Japan virtually at will with only the remote chance of effective opposition.

A quartet of XXI Bomber Command B-29s passes over the Kure Naval Arsenal in the course of an attack on 22 June 1945. Note the bomb explosions in the water.

World War II variants

Back in the USA, production of the B-29 was well under way by the early summer of 1945, and some eight aircraft were coming off the production lines every day. But so successful was the basic B-29 initial model that there was little need for the extensive development that characterised most other major combat aircraft of World War II.

The first major modification was essentially experimental, and involved the conversion of the first YB-29 to an inline-engine powerplant. This conversion was carried out by General Motors, and the revised powerplant consisted of four Allison V-3420-11 liquid-cooled inlines. Extensively tested as the **XB-39**, this aircraft offered no significant improvement over the basic B-29 series, so production was not contemplated.

Experience over Germany had given the USAAF a healthy respect for head-on attacks by cannon-armed fighters against heavy bomber formations, and by 1943 it was considered desirable to boost the defensive firepower of the B-29s against the possibility of the Japanese adopting such a tactic. So B-29s from block number 40 (B-29-40 onwards) were provided with a four-gun forward dorsal turret. No special designation was associated with this alteration, but it was also incorporated in the only production variant of the Superfortress in World War II, the **B-29A-BN** built solely by the Boeing-run government facility at Renton. However, the major difference between the B-29A and the basic B-29 was the revised wing of the former, which was increased in span by 1 ft (0.305 m) and had a different centre section. Whereas that of the B-29 had been a two-piece structure bolted together and

fitted as a unit with the join on the centreline, that of the B-29A was a single unit of considerably less span, projecting only slightly from the sides of the fuselage. The B-29's centre section extended outboard as far as the juncture with the outer wing panels, and included the mountings for the engines; that of the B-29A required intermediate panels, between the centre-section stub and the outer panels, with the mountings for the engines. The B-29A was also to have had revised engine nacelles of better aerodynamic shape, with the oil coolers and intercooler in each unit moved farther aft to permit the virtual deletion of the 'chin'. These 'chinless' nacelles were nicknamed 'Andy Gump' nacelles after a celebrated chinless comic-strip character, but were not fitted to wartime B-29As.

The designation **B-29B** was also used in World War II, but applied only to conversions rather than new-build aircraft. LeMay's tactical revisions of 1945 had rendered defensive armament all but superfluous, and most in-service B-29s had their dorsal and ventral turrets, plus associated equipment and gunners, removed to improve low-altitude speed and permit an increased bomb-load. The tail turret was retained to provide token defence and to maintain the centre of gravity in the right position. These alterations were normally effected in the field, but 311 Bell-built aircraft to this standard were produced in the USA. At the same time the rear defence was improved by the addition of AN/APG-15B radar-directed fire control for the rear turret. This simple system detected any aircraft approaching the B-29B from the rear and laid the gun automatically, leaving the gunner

Above: General Electric barbette in the rear dorsal position. The paired 0.5-in (12.7-mm) guns each had 1,000 rounds of ammunition, and the barbette was remotely controlled by the gunner in the low-drag blister in front of the installation. This gunner had sole control of the barbette, and was the tactical co-ordinator for all defensive firepower.
Below: The four-gun forward dorsal barbette of the B-29A series, controlled primarily by the bombardier.
Right: Nose view of a B-29A. In the very forward portion of the nose sat the bombardier, controlling the four- and two-gun forward dorsal and ventral barbettes, with the pilots behind him.

merely to make the decision whether or not to engage. The aerodynamic and weight improvements associated with the B-29B conversion boosted the maximum speed of the variant to 364 mph (586 km/h) at 25,000 ft (7,620 m), suiting the aircraft admirably for reconnaissance work and special hit-and-run missions.

Another modification, and one that received no special designation, also involved the deletion of all but the tail armament. This was the special version of the Superfortress used by the 315th Bombardment Wing, which was based on Guam and tasked with precision raids on Japanese oil refineries. The sighting aid used in this role was the AN/APQ-7 radar bomb sight, whose antenna was carried in a 14-ft (4.27-m) wing-shaped fairing under the fuselage.

Other types of Superfortress used in World War II were also conversions from existing bomber airframes, and there were also a number of experimental models that should be recorded, for though the designation B-29B was the ultimate allocated to wartime production, development of other derivatives was well advanced and progressed into the post-war period.

B-29C was the designation provisionally allocated to a single B-29 which was to have been fitted with improved versions of the not altogether satisfactory R-3350 radial, but the plan was cancelled and the designation was not reallocated. A similar fate befell the **B-29D**, the proposed designation of a radically improved B-29 series of much stronger alloy construction and powered by Pratt & Whitney R-4360 radials. When it was seen how different the aircraft was becoming, the revised basic designation B-50 was deemed fit, and there were thus no B-29Ds.

The **XB-29E** was a single B-29

Left: The sole XB-29G was used most beneficially as a test-bed for the early generation of American turbojets. The whole turbojet fitting could be retracted into the revised bomb bay.
Below left: Tested in July 1944 was this experimental installation of twin Emerson barbettes, located as power-operated fittings on the nose of a B-29.
Below: Another possibility flight tested in July 1944 was this revised rear-fuselage armament, comprising a Sperry ball turret in the rear ventral position, a Martin turret in the rear dorsal position, and single manually-operated 0.5-in (12.7-mm) Browning guns as waist guns on each beam.
Bottom: At the tail of the much-modified B-29-BW serialled 224441 (42-24441) was a General Electric turret with two 0.5-in (12.7-mm) Browning machine-guns.

modified to test various aspects of the defensive fire-control system designed for the B-29 series, and was extensively used in 1946 to assess many of the features which had been accepted with little reservation in World War II but which were thought to be in need of further examination when the pressure of combat was off. The designation **XB-29H** was given to a single B-29A also used for armament trials, this time in 1947 with outsize bombs and other special offensive stores.

For some time it was thought that B-29s could perhaps be based in Alaska, where equipment for cold-weather operations was vitally necessary. Six B-29-BWs were therefore 'winterised' for trials purposes, but on the completion of the trials the **B-29F** aircraft were reconverted to standard configuration. One of the most important B-29 conversions produced the sole **XB-29G**, adapted from the airframe of a B-29-BA (44-84043) and very profitably used as an engine test-bed for the new turbojet powerplants on which so many USAAF hopes rested in the immediate post-war period. This aircraft was fitted with a special retractable rig in the bomb bay, so that test engines (notably the J35, J47 and J73) could be extended into the slipstream once the XB-29G was airborne and run in realistic conditions. Finally, among this initial series of B-29 modifications, was the **YB-29J**, a designation applied to six B-29 aircraft converted as a service-test batch to prove the revised 'Andy Gump' nacelles and fuel-injected R-3350-CA-2 engines intended for late-production B-29As.

Enola Gay and Bock's Car

While these and other modifications to the basic type were being planned, built and operated, the Superfortress opened a new phase in world history. As noted above, the Japanese could not envisage defeat despite the rapid destruction of their armed forces and war-making industries during 1944 and early 1945. The Americans were thus faced with the prospect of invading Japan, a military operation estimated by even the most optimistic planners as entailing American casualties of several hundreds of thousands. But there was an alternative

available by the middle of 1945, in the form of the atomic bomb successfully tested at Alamogordo on 16 July 1945. The possibility of using such a weapon had already been considered by US planners, and earlier in 1944 the USAAF had formed under the command of Colonel Paul W. Tibbets Jr the 509th Composite Group as part of the 315th (Very Heavy) Bombardment Wing. The mission entrusted to the relevant 393rd (Very Heavy) Bombardment Squadron was exceptionally thorough training in the accurate delivery of single large

stores from high altitude. In 1945 the unit moved to Tinian in the Marianas Islands, and flew several practice raids against the Japanese islands.

The political decision to use atomic weapons was finally made by President Truman, and on 6 August 1945 Tibbets led the first nuclear raid of history, the target being Hiroshima. The strike force consisted of the B-29-45-MO *Enola Gay* (44-86292) in the markings of a reconnaissance aircraft and carrying the 9,700-lb (4,400-kg) 'Little Boy' atomic bomb, supported by a reserve aircraft, two more B-29s with observers, and three weather reconnaissance Superfortresses. All bombardiers

were capable of dropping a bomb from high altitude either visually with the Norden bombsight or electronically with radar into a circle of 500-ft (152-m) diameter, and on this occasion the *Enola Gay*'s bombardier dropped from an altitude of 31,600 ft (9,630 m) with great accuracy: the 'Little Boy' exploded 800 ft (245 m) above the aim point and 4.7 square miles of Hiroshima ceased to exist.

The Japanese were stunned by the catastrophe, and quite unable to come to grips with the implications of the new technology. So on 9 August the terrible lesson had to be repeated. This time the Superfortress with the atomic weapon was *Bock's Car* (painted on the nose as *Bockscar*) flown by Major Charles W. Sweeney, and the target was the city of Nagasaki, whose centre was largely destroyed by the 'Fat Boy' weapon. So forceful was this repeated lesson that the Japanese immediately made clear their desire to surrender, so bringing World War II to an end. For Boeing this was a mixed blessing: more than 2,000 Super-fortresses had been delivered to the USAAF, and production was to reach 3,974 before the last production line, that at Renton, closed down in May 1946. But with the end of the war, some 5,092 Superfortresses currently on order were cancelled. In the hands of the 20th Air Force Superfortresses had dropped some 169,676 tons of bombs (62 per cent of them incendiaries) and many thousands of mines, suffering 414 combat losses and another 105 written off after landing, giving the 20th Air Force a VJ-Day strength of about 1,100 B-29s of all marks.

Below: The most famous of all B-29s is *Enola Gay*, a B-29-MO serialled 44-86292 and used for the first atomic bombing raid in history. The aircraft is seen making a low pass, and is now preserved as part of the National Air and Space Museum in Washington, DC.
Inset below: The other B-29 to drop an atomic weapon was *Bock's Car*, whose highly appropriate nose art is seen here. These two aircraft must be credited as having achieved more destruction than any other single aircraft in history.

Other Developments

Some Superfortress developments have already been mentioned, but these were mostly experimental. Other developments, both during and after World War II, were of an operational nature, and designed to facilitate the primary deployment of the Superfortress as a long-range heavy bomber. This became particularly important after the war, for the B-17 and B-24 were rapidly phased out as front-line bombers, leaving the uniquely capable Superfortress as the USA's primary strategic weapon until the advent of jet bombers, notably the Boeing B-47 Stratojet.

The first of these special-purpose Superfortresses was the **F-13**, initially a single B-29-BW converted for photographic reconnaissance, a role in which the speed, range and ceiling of the B-29 were very useful attributes. This first conversion, which did not impair the basic aircraft's offensive and defensive capabilities, was rapidly proved successful, and another 117 aircraft (B-29s and B-29As) were similarly modified. The standard fit comprised one K-17B, one K-18 and two K-22 cameras in the fuselage and forward bomb bay, though others could be carried as specific missions demanded. Extra fuel tankage could also be accommodated in the bomb bays for very long-range missions. Converted aircraft were designated F-13 or **F-13A** depending on whether a B-29 or B-29A was the origin of the conversion, and the first such aircraft became operational with the 1st Squadron of the 311th Photographic Reconnaissance Wing in the Pacific theatre during December 1944. In 1948 surviving aircraft were redesignated **RB-29** and **RB-29A**.

The initial deployment of the Superfortress to China and the Pacific, where long overwater flights rapidly became the norm, raised the question of how best to recover crews who had to ditch their aircraft as a result of mechanical failure or combat damage. A partial answer was found in the development of the 'Superdumbo', a B-29 equipped with survival and rescue gear which accompanied the main bomber formations and diverted to assist any crew forced to ditch. (The 'Dumbo' was a similarly equipped version of the B-17, which was a useful aircraft in its own right, but lacked the performance in speed and range to accompany the Superfortress raids.) After World War II the Superdumbo was further developed as the **SB-29**, with an A-3 lifeboat carried under the fuselage for air-dropping. Some 16 conversions to SB-29 standard were effected.

Another conversion to facilitate the operation of B-29s in the primary bomber role resulted in the **WB-29**, a specialised weather reconnaissance variant. This was used for long-range reconnoitring of B-29 raid routes for adverse weather conditions.

In April 1947 the US Navy received four B-29s surplus to USAAF requirements. These were allocated the basic designation P2B, and were obtained initially as platforms for use in a number of naval long-range anti-submarine and surface-search programmes. In this guise the aircraft were distinguishable by the ventral radomes for the experimental electronics carried. Two of the aircraft (84028, ex-USAAF 45-21789 and 84029, ex-USAF 45-21787) were **P2B-1S** aircraft, the second becoming the launch aircraft for the Bell D-558-II rocket-powered supersonic research aircraft. The other pair (84030, ex-USAF

45-21791 and 84031, ex-USAF 44-87766) were designated **P2B-2S**.

Perhaps the most important development undertaken with the B-29 series was the technique of inflight-refuelling. Such a technique had long been envisaged and indeed tried, but the techniques for the 1920s and 1930s had been rudimentary, requiring skilled crews, fair weather and a

Above left: The Superfortress serialled 521717 (45-21717) began life as a standard B-29-BW bomber of Boeing Wichita's last production batch, but after World War II was modified as a WB-29 weather reconnaissance aircraft.
Top: Another off the Boeing Wichita line, this B-29 was converted into an SB-29 'Superdumbo' rescue aircraft, fitted to paradrop a special lifeboat to crews which had been forced to ditch.
Above: Under the designation P2B-1S, two B-29-BW aircraft were used after World War II by the US Navy for a variety of experimental purposes, including the air-launch of supersonic research aircraft such as the Douglas D-558-II illustrated.
Left: Long-range B-29B *Pacusan Dreamboat*.

great degree of luck: in general, a hose lowered from the tanker aircraft had to be grappled by the receiving aircraft, and the two aircraft had then to formate for a protracted period as the fuel was slowly transferred. The increase in long-range operations during World War II raised demands for an effective system of inflight-refuelling for use by standard crews, and this tendency was

reinforced after World War II, when the USA in particular was faced by the prospect of very long-range strategic operations from bases in US territory.

The range capability of the Superfortress was dramatically demonstrated by a world-record distance flight in November 1945, when the stripped-out B-29B *Pacusan Dreamboat*, fitted with extra fuel tankage and 'Andy

Gump' nacelles, flew nonstop from Guam to Washington, DC. The flight covered 8,198 miles (13,193 km) in 35 hours, but the need to remove all military equipment served to highlight the fact that combat operations over these distances, which would certainly be entailed in operations against the USSR, could only be undertaken with the aid of inflight-refuelling.

American thoughts turned first to the British looped-hose system, raised to a practical level by Flight Refuelling Ltd. The designations initially associated with US adoption of the system were **B-29K** and **B-29L**, referring respectively to tanker and receiver aircraft. However, by the time that conversions started at the specially reopened Plant 2 at Wichita, the aircraft had been redesignated, and the K suffix then went to a single B-29-BW modified for cargo transport as the **CB-29K**. As finalised by Boeing, the inflight-refuelling system pioneered for the Superfortress consisted of two portions: the **KB-29M** tanker and the **B-29MR** receiver aircraft.

The KB-29M, of which 92 were produced in a conversion programme launched in 1948, consisted of a standard B-29 airframe modified to accommodate a long hose on a power-driven reel in the rear of the fuselage, and two jettisonable fuel tanks, each holding about 2,300 US gal (8,706 litres) of fuel, in the bomb bays; these tanks were interconnected with the aircraft's fuel system, so that

this fuel too could be transferred when required.

The procedure was for the tanker and receiver aircraft to fly in formation, the former above and ahead of the latter. The tanker then extended a hauling line, which was caught by a grapnel on the end of a contact line trailed by the receiver aircraft in a cross-over manoeuvre and then hauled in by a winch on board the receiver aircraft, where the receiver operator ensured that the two lines were close up against the mouth of the fuel receptacle. He then detached the contact line and attached the hauling line to the winch, which pulled in the hauling line and the hose attached to it; the hose nozzle was then connected to the receptacle on the starboard side of the rear fuselage under the tailplane, and locked by hydraulic toggles. Fuel could then be pumped into the 2,500-US gal (9,464-litre) tank in the B-29MR's aft bomb bay, this tank being plumbed into the conventional fuel tankage system. A previously set pull on the hose would then ensure the detachment of the hose, which could be

reeled back into the tanker aircraft. Conversions of B-29s into B-29MR aircraft totalled 74.

A considerable amount of operational evaluation proved the feasibility of the system, but also its limitations in terms of the time required for the two aircraft to link up, the slow rate of fuel transfer and the low airspeed imposed on the two aircraft by the flexing of the hose in the slipstream. So Boeing set to work to evolve a more satisfactory system, evolved as the company's patented 'flying boom'. This was a rigid and telescopic arm pivoted to the undersurface of the tanker aircraft's rear fuselage and 'flown' by a single operator in the previous tail turret, from where he controlled the aerodynamic butterfly (Vee) flying surfaces at the tip of the boom. With these controls the operator could deploy and extend the boom, and then fly its tip into the receptacle in the upper surface of the receiver aircraft's fuselage. A panel of lights on the belly of the tanker was connected to the boom in such a way that automatic instructions were provided to the pilot of the receiver aircraft

pioneered on the KB-29P, of which 116 were produced at Renton by conversion of bombers such as this B-29A in 1950–51. *Right:* A KB-29P passes fuel to a Republic F-84 tactical fighter via the receptacle in the fighter's port wing.

for the maintenance of the correct position relative to the tanker.

The hose method had first been envisaged for the B-29 force in November 1947, with trials beginning in March 1948 with water and in May 1948 with fuel. Such was the urgency attached to the inflight-refuelling programme that it was in May 1948 that Boeing proposed the superior flying boom system and only 12 months later that the first trials were started, using converted YB-29J aircraft. As noted above, these aircraft had been produced to test the power-plant installation for the late-block B-29A series. With this series curtailed, most of the YB-29Js were modified to F-13A/RB-29A standard under the designation **RB-29J**. But two aircraft (44-86398 and 44-86402) were modified to test the flying-boom system under the designation **YKB-29J**. The evaluation proved the general superiority of the system over the looped-hose type, and the US Air Force contracted with Boeing for the provision of 40 aircraft converted to this standard under the designation **KB-29P**. The conversions were

carried out at the Renton plant, part of which had already been reopened for production of the C-97A (a magnificent freighter-tanker series evolved from the Model 345), and in 1950 and 1951 Renton completed a total of 116 KB-29P conversions.

Most of the KB-29Ps had the standard flying boom system, but some were fitted with a flexible probe-and-drogue appendix to the boom, trials having shown that it was easier for tactical aircraft (notably short-range fighters with turbojet engines) to close up towards the tanker and insert a fixed probe into a trailing drogue. Several B-29 conversions were made in the UK by Flight Refuelling Ltd under contract to the USAAF and USAF, the most important being the lone **YKB-29T**, converted from the KB-29M serialled 45-21734 with three-point probe-and-drogue refuelling capability to allow the simultaneous refuelling of three fighters, one under the tail and the other pair under the wingtips. Compared with the KB-29M series, the KB-29P had increased transferrable fuel capacity, and all armament was removed.

It cannot be denied, however, that the Superfortress was not particularly effective in the inflight-refuelling role: the fighters and bombers entering service in the early 1950s were sluggish on the controls at the B-29 series' maximum speed, and so the Superfortress was not really compatible with the current generation of combat aircraft. Even so, the type is of importance as the real pioneer of inflight-refuelling. Other ways in which the type was used in the early 1950s and before were as the **TB-29** trainer, the **QB-29** drone and the **EB-29B**, this last being used as a television relay station and as the launch platform for the extraordinary McDonnell XF-85 Goblin air-launched fighter, designed to be carried as protection by Convair B-36 bombers on long-range penetration missions.

In the late 1940s the RAF found itself without an adequate long-range bomber pending deliveries of the Avro Lincoln. In March 1950, therefore, the USAF loaned the RAF 88 B-29s: these served until 1955 under the designation **Washington B. Mk 1**.

Swansong

In 1946 the USAAF had some 30 bombardment groups equipped with the Superfortress. Nothing like this number were allocated to the Strategic Air Command on its activation in that year, largely as a result of the USAAF's rapid demobilisation. Numbers of B-29s in front-line service declined slowly as more modern equipment came into service; nonetheless when the Korean War broke out in 1950 many groups were still equipped with the Superfortress. During the Korean War five groups equipped with the Superfortress (the 19th, 22nd, 92nd, 98th and 307th Bombardment Groups) operated in support of the UN forces, largely in the medium-level interdiction role. In 37 months of the Korean War B-29s dropped 167,100 tons of bombs in about 21,000 sorties, losing 34 aircraft in combat. Legend had it that the Superfortresses were easy prey for the communists' Mikoyan-Gurevich MiG-15 fighters, but this is not so, as the statistical record indicates: only 16 B-29s were lost to enemy fighters, while the bombers' gunners claimed 33 fighters certainly destroyed, 17 probably destroyed and a further 11 damaged. More importantly, however, the B-29s were generally successful in their allotted tasks, which frequently included bombing such heavily defended targets as road and rail bridges, marshalling yards, power-generating facilities and equipment dumps. In all, the B-29s operated on every day of the Korean War but 26, playing a vital part in the final success of

UN operations.

It was clear, however, that the days of the Superfortress were numbered. Modern fighters had a considerable edge in terms of speed and firepower, and in any event the US Air Force had newer and better bombers in service and under development. The B-29 was slowly relegated to second-line duties, and the type made its last operational sortie on 21 June 1960, a B-29-MO of the 6023rd Radar Evaluation Squadron flying a routine mission from its base in Okinawa.

Boeing Model 345-2

From a time relatively early in the career of the Superfortress it had been clear that the type was limited by two basic factors: the structure of the airframe and the power/reliability ratio of its engine. The former was conditioned by the types of light alloy available at the time the B-29 was designed, and limited maximum take-off weights, payload and the like; the latter again reflected the state of the art in the early 1940s, but it must also be admitted that the R-3350 radial had problems throughout its life, and was notable for its tendency to burst into flames. One attempt to find an alternative powerplant, in the form of the Allison V-3420 tested in the XB-39 version, has already been mentioned. This engine was essentially a pair of V-1710 inlines coupled to a common propeller shaft, and provided an output that fell gradually from 2,600 hp (1,940 kW) at take-off to 2,100 hp (1,567 kW) at 25,000 ft (7,620 m). Tests with the XB-39 proved that the new engine provided some advantages, notably a speed increase to 405 mph (652 km/h) at 35,000 ft (10,670 m), but that in overall terms performance was not improved by a margin sufficiently great to warrant the total disruption of the production

The B-50D was the ultimate offensive development of the Superfortress series. Well displayed here are the twin bomb bays with the radome for the bombing radar between them, and the much revised nacelles associated with the Pratt & Whitney R-4360 radials of the type. This was the 15th B-50D, and the last built without a receptacle for the 'flying boom' type of inflight-refuelling. It is worth noting that while the unit cost of a B-29 had been US$639,188 (airframe US$399,541, powerplant US$109,194, ordnance US$95,715 and electronics US$34,738) that of the fully developed B-50D was US$1,444,300. The aircraft illustrated is in its later configuration as the last of 11 TB-50D conversions with 'K' radar.

programme that would be entailed.

The massive 18-cylinder Pratt & Whitney R-4360 Wasp Major radial offered more promise. In 1944, therefore, Pratt & Whitney were instructed to proceed with the development of the Superfortress with this powerplant, and were allocated a B-29A (42-93845) on which to evolve a definitive powerplant installation. For this role the aircraft was designated **XB-44**, and such was the control exercised over the project by the engine manufacturer that in some documents the XB-44 was described as a Pratt & Whitney rather than a Boeing aircraft. So successful was the conversion, in terms of reliability and improved performance, that orders were placed for 200 production examples of the XB-44 in June 1945, the series designation **B-29D** being allocated.

But the B-29D was not just the basic B-29 with R-4360 engines. Boeing had also revised the airframe on the basis of a structure of 75 ST aluminium alloy in place of the earlier 24 ST. This meant, for example, that the wing was some 600 lb (272 kg) lighter than that of earlier B-29s but also some 16 per cent stronger, and thus better able to deal with the 60 per cent greater power offered by the R-4360 radials, each rated at about 3,500 hp (2,611 kW). All previous Superfortress models had been evolved under the basic Model 345 company designation, but for the B-29D Boeing rightly decided on an updated designation, **Model 345-2**.

No production had been started, however, when the great order cancellations that followed VJ-Day in September 1945 reduced orders for the B-29D to a mere 60 aircraft.

Boeing B-50

In December 1945 the B-29D was redesignated **B-50**, as part of a successful attempt by the USAAF to retain the type in production at a time when hundreds of B-29s were being cocooned in plastic as part of a long-term storage system. The USAAF correctly reasoned that the new designation would help to remove the type's origins from the minds of Congressional opponents to continued military spending.

Whatever the reasons, a new designation for the B-29D was fully justified, for the aircraft retained only some 25 per cent commonality with earlier variants of the Superfortress series. As noted above, the whole powerplant installation was different, and neatly engineered by Pratt & Whitney; and the aircraft structure was thoroughly different thanks to the availability of the new alloy. But Boeing had made a number of other alterations, the most obvious of which was a much larger vertical tail, a feature that had been flight proved on a B-29-BW (42-24528) retained at Seattle for just such purposes. An unusual feature of this taller tail was the fact that it folded down at the top to permit the aircraft's hangarage in standard USAAF hangars. The certainty of higher speeds and greater weights at take-off and landing were compensated by an increase in the area of the flaps. Further improvements worked into the Model 345-2 design were: hydraulic rudder boost and nose-wheel steering; upgraded landing gear to cater for higher weights; electrical de-icing of the pilot's windscreen, thermal de-icing of the wings and tail unit by means of hollow-wall leading-edge structures through which was pumped hot gas from combustion heaters on each of the inner pair of engines and at the bottom of the fin; and reversible-pitch propellers to help halt the aircraft on wet runways. All in all, the Model 345-2 represented a markedly improved aircraft in comparison with the Model 345 series.

It was thought unnecessary to trouble with a prototype, and the first B-50 was a production aircraft of the initial series, the **B-50A Superfortress** (designated **Model 345-21-1** by Boeing), 60 being built to the initial reduced order for B-29Ds. The first of these flew on 25 June 1947, and 59 were completed as bombers while one was retained by Boeing as a development aircraft under the designation **YB-50C**. This aircraft, actually the last of the first B-50A series, was not completed. It was to have been the prototype for the ultimate development of the Superfortress series, the **B-54**. This was planned with a maximum take-off weight of 207,000 lb (93,895 kg), a longer fuselage and greater-span wing, and power provided by four R-4360-51 turbo-compound radials. Orders for 14 **B-54A** bomber and 29 **RB-54A** reconnaissance aircraft had been placed before the project was abandoned in April 1949.

The B-50As had been in service only a short time when 57 of them were cycled through the Boeing Wichita plant for conversion with inflight-refuelling receptacles. In this form the aircraft were intended to operate alongside the newly formed KB-29M tanker force, and it was a B-50A that made the first non-stop aerial circumnavigation of the Earth in March 1949, covering 23,452 miles (37,741 km) in 94 hours with the aid of four inflight-refuellings from pairs of KB-29M tankers. Total production of the B-50A was 79, and of these 11 became unarmed **TB-50A** crew trainers for the B-36 programme while the others were modified as three-point probe-and-drogue tankers, under the designation **KB-50J**, for deployment in association with the short-range fighters deployed by the Tactical Air Command.

The next Superfortress variant was the **B-50B**, basically similar to the B-50A apart from structural alterations that permitted a maximum take-off weight of 170,000 lb (77,112 kg) compared with 140,000 lb (63,504 kg) for the B-50A. Total B-50B procurement was 45 aircraft, of which 44 were delivered as bombers in 1949. The first of the batch was retained by Boeing as a development aircraft under the designation **EB-50B**, and at one stage was fitted with tracked landing gear. The 44 B-50Bs were soon cycled through Wichita to become **RB-50B** reconnaissance aircraft, with provision for a special pod (containing optical and electronic equipment plus its operators) in the rear bomb bay. During the modification process the aircraft were given inflight-refuelling receptacles and one 700-US gal (2,650-litre) auxiliary fuel tank under each outer wing panel. The aircraft were extensively modified in a variety of reconnaissance configurations later in their careers: 14 became **RB-50E** special photographic reconnaissance aircraft, 14 more were turned into **RB-50F** special-mission machines with SHORAN (SHOrt-RAnge Navigation) radar, and 15 became **RB-50G** platforms similar to the RB-50Fs except for additional radar (distinguishable by the RB-50G's five radomes), the nose of the B-50D, extra armament and a crew of 16. All surviving aircraft were later taken in hand by Hayes Industries for conversion into KB-50J three-point tactical tankers. In this conversion the tail of each aircraft was lengthened by some 6 ft (1.83 m), and apart from the

Above left: All in-service B-50B bombers were in 1947 converted by Boeing Wichita into RB-50B strategic reconnaissance aircraft with a special mission capsule in the rear bomb bay, two 700-US gal (2,650-litre) tanks under the wings, and provision for looped-hose refuelling by means of a receptacle visible just aft of the tail bumper.
Above: Serial number 7098 (47-098) was the lead article of the second B-50A batch, and is seen here as a 15th Air Force bomber with looped-hose receiver.
Left: The first B-50A (46-002) is moved out for a flight test in June 1947. The series was to have been built at Renton as B-50A-BN, but in fact came from the Seattle Plant 2 as B-50A-BO.
Below: All KB-50JS were conversions.

three hose units (under the tail and just inboard of the wingtips), the most notable alteration was the addition of a pair of 5,200-lb (2,359-kg) thrust General Electric J47 turbojets in pods under the wings in the positions previously occupied by the auxiliary fuel tanks. These extra engines boosted the maximum speed of the KB-50J to 444 mph (715 km/h) at 17,000 ft (5,180 m), so making the tankers more compatible in terms of speed with the fighters they had to refuel.

The most important variant of the B-50 series was the **B-50D**, designated **Model 345-9-6** by Boeing and first flown on 23 May 1949. It was this variant which introduced the underwing auxiliary tanks, but the most apparent change was the one-piece Plexiglass nose with an optically flat panel for the bombardier. All previous models had been produced with a seven-piece nose cone. The operational capability of the B-50D was also enhanced by provision of a single-point refuelling system and a receptacle for the flying boom type of inflight-refuelling tanker, and it should be noted that each of the underwing tanks could be replaced on short-range missions by a single 4,000-lb (1,814-kg) bomb. Production of the B-50D reached 222 units, largely as a response to the steady deterioration of relations with the Soviet Union. By 1950 the type had been categorised as the most important medium bombardment aircraft in the SAC inventory. Subsequent modification of the B-50D produced 11 **TB-50D** trainers for use in the preparation of B-36 crews, and these 11 aircraft later joined 101 B-50Ds in the conversion programme for KB-50 tankers, subsequently identified as KB-50J aircraft. Other B-50Ds became **WB-50D** weather reconnaissance aircraft, and one **DB-50D** was used for dropping trials with the GAM-63 Rascal stand-off missile.

The final new-build Super-fortress variant was the **TB-50H**, identified by Boeing as the **Model 345-31-26**. This was a specialised radar-bombing trainer without armament but fitted with the 'K' navigation/bombing system developed for the B-47. Delivered in 1952 and 1953, the TB-50H trainers had the 'K' system equipment in the rear bomb bay, and fuselage stations were provided for an instructor and two pupils. The variant was intended for short-range training flights, and thus had no provision for inflight-refuelling; the variant was also very light, at 120,000 lb (54,432 kg), and was thus the fastest piston-engine Super-fortress type with a maximum speed of 418 mph (673 km/h) at 31,000 ft (9,450 m). Some of the TB-50H aircraft later became **WB-50H** weather reconnaissance machines, and all were ultimately converted into **KB-50K** three-point tankers.

Various types of B-50 were used in Korea for bombing, reconnaissance and refuelling,

Above: Reconfigured as a TB-50D for the Convair B-36 programme, the B-50D lost its barbetted armament, while internal alterations provided accommodation for two pupils and one instructor, a radar bombing system, and a rear bomb bay packed with special electronics. The TB-50Ds later became WB-50D weather reconnaissance platforms.
Left: The first B-50B was retained by Boeing for experimental work under the designation EB-50B, and one experiment replaced the conventional wheels with tracked bogies.
Right: Little differentiated the flight-deck of the B-50A from that of the B-29 series. But that of the later B-50 had considerably less framing in the extreme nose, improving forward vision.

but by the late 1950s the concept of the type was obsolete, and the last tankers and weather reconnaissance versions were phased out in the mid-1960s, though the KB-50 variants had a last campaign at the very beginning of the Vietnam war, operating as emergency low-level tankers for tactical aircraft.

By the end of the 1960s, therefore, the B-29 and B-50 Superfortress had passed into history. But in another form the type survived into the early 1980s. During World War II,

several B-29s force-landed in Russian-held territory and were interned. Impressed by the technical achievement represented by the Superfortress, and at last realising the significance of strategic bombing in modern warfare, the Russians determined to copy the B-29, though they possessed virtually none of the relevant technology. In a programme prodigious by any standards, and which could only be attempted by a totalitarian regime, the Russians achieved a new miracle, flying their first

Tupolev Tu-4 in 1947. Outwardly, the only difference between the Russian Tu-4 and the American B-29 was the former's defensive armament of five pairs of 20-mm cannon. In all, some 1,200 Tu-4s were built, and the type served with Long-Range Aviation until supplanted by Tu-16s and Tu-20s in the late 1950s. The Tupolev design bureau also developed a transport version, identified as the **Tu-70** and using the wings, tail unit and landing gear of the Tu-4 with a new fuselage for up to 66 passengers. In the event Aeroflot decided to concentrate its post-war efforts on medium-range commercial operations, and only the prototype Tu-70 was built. Other developments were the **Tu-75** military transport with a rear ramp and two ventral hatches for paratroop operations, and the **Tu-80** development aircraft based on the Tu-4 but with a fuselage similar to that of the Tu-85. Only one example each of the Tu-75 and Tu-80 were built, flying in 1950 and 1949 respectively. The final expression of the Tu-4 design was the scaled-up **Tu-85** heavy bomber of 1949: this was a true giant of the period, with a defensive armament of 10 23-mm cannon, an offensive load of 44,092 lb (20,000 kg) and a maximum take-off weight of 235,891 lb (107,000 kg) lifted by four 4,300-hp (3,208-kW) Dobynin VD-K4 radials for a maximum speed of 410 mph (660 km/h) at 32,810 ft (10,000 m) and a range of 8,078 miles (13,000 km).

About 400 Tu-4s were handed over to the Communist Chinese regime in the 1950s, and these still provided the main long-range bombardment force of the Red Chinese air force in the early 1980s. Even though it reflects sadly on the Chinese air arm that it operates such elderly equipment, it is nonetheless an eloquent testimony to the greatness of Boeing's original design.

Specifications

B-29 Superfortress

Type: long-range heavy bomber

Accommodation: 10–14

Armament: (offensive) up to 20,000 lb (9,072 kg) of bombs (defensive) two 0.5-in (12.7-mm) machine-guns in each of four barbettes, and two 0.5-in (12.7-mm) machine-guns and one 20-mm cannon in tail turret

Powerplant: four 2,200-hp (1,641-kw) Wright R-3350-23 turbocharged radial piston engines

Performance:
maximum speed 358 mph (576 km/h) at 25,000 ft (7,620 m)
cruising speed 230 mph (370 km/h)
initial climb rate 38 minutes to 20,000 ft (6,095 m)
service ceiling 31,850 ft (9,710 m)
range 5,600 miles (9,010 km)

Weights:
empty equipped 70,140 lb (31,816 kg)
normal take-off 124,000 lb (56,250 kg)
maximum take-off 138,000 lb (62,597 kg)

Dimensions:
span 141 ft 3 in (43.05 m)
length 99 ft (30.18 m)
height 29 ft 7 in (9.01 m)
wing area 1,736 sq ft (161.27 m²)

B-29A Superfortress

Type: long-range heavy bomber

Accommodation: 10–14

Armament: (offensive) as for B-29 (defensive) as for B-29 except four guns in forward dorsal barbette

Powerplant: four 2,200-hp (1,641-kw) Wright R-3350-57 turbocharged radial piston engines

Performance:
maximum speed 358 mph (576 km/h) at 25,000 ft (7,620 m)
cruising speed 230 mph (370 km/h)
initial climb rate 38 minutes to 20,000 ft (6,095 m)
service ceiling 31,850 ft (9,710 m)
range 6,500 miles (10,460 km)

Weights:
empty equipped 71,360 lb (32,369 kg)
normal take-off —
maximum take-off 141,100 lb (64,003 kg)

Dimensions:
span 142 ft 3 in (43.36 m)
length 99 ft (30.18 m)
height 29 ft 7 in (9.01 m)
wing area —

B-29B Superfortress

Type: long-range heavy bomber

Accommodation: 8–10

Armament: (offensive) as for B-29 (defensive) two 0.5-in (12.7-mm) machine-guns and one 20-mm cannon in Bell tail turret with AN/APG-15B radar fire control

Powerplant: four 2,200-hp (1,641-kw) Wright R-3350-59 turbocharged radial piston engines

Performance:
maximum speed 364 mph (586 km/h) at 25,000 ft (7,620 m)
cruising speed 228 mph (367 km/h)
initial climb rate 38 minutes to 20,000 ft (6,095 m)
service ceiling 32,000 ft (9,755 m)
range 6,700 miles (10,780 km)

Weights:
empty equipped 69,000 lb (31,298 kg)
normal take-off —
maximum take-off 137,500 lb (62,370 kg)

Dimensions:
span as for B-29
length
height
wing area

KB-29P Superfortress

Type: inflight-refuelling tanker

Accommodation: 10

Armament: none

Powerplant: four 2,200-hp (1,641-kw) Wright R-3350-23 turbocharged radial piston engines (typical)

Performance:
maximum speed 400 mph (644 km/h) at 30,000 ft (9,145 m)
cruising speed 315 mph (507 km/h)
initial climb rate 500 ft (152 m) per minute
service ceiling 38,000 ft (11,580 m)
range 2,300 miles (3,700 km)

Weights:
empty equipped 69,011 lb (31,303 kg)
normal take-off —
maximum take-off 138,500 lb (62,824 kg)

Dimensions:
span 141 ft 3 in (43.05 m)
length 120 ft 1 in (36.60 m)
height 29 ft 7 in (9.01 m)
wing area 1,736 sq ft (161.27 m²)

B-50A Superfortress

Type: medium strategic bomber

Accommodation: 12

Armament: (offensive) up to 20,000 lb (9,072 kg) of bombs (defensive) 10 0.5-in (12.7-mm) machine-guns in three two-gun barbette, plus one 20-mm cannon and two 0.5-in (12.7-mm) guns in tail turret

Powerplant: four 3,500-hp (2,611-kw) Pratt & Whitney R-4360-35 turbocharged radial piston engines

Performance:
maximum speed 385 mph (620 km/h) at 25,000 ft (7,620 m)
cruising speed 235 mph (378 km/h)
initial climb rate 2,225 ft (678 m) per minute
service ceiling 37,000 ft (11,280 m)
range 4,650 miles (7,485 km)

Weight:
empty equipped 81,050 lb (36,764 kg)
normal take-off —
maximum take-off 168,708 lb (76,526 kg)

Dimensions:
span 141 ft 3 in (43.05 m)
length 99 ft (30.18 m)
height 32 ft 8 in (9.96 m)
wing area 1,720 sq ft (159.79 m²)

B-50D Superfortress

Type: medium strategic bomber

Accommodation: 11

Armament: (offensive) up to 28,000 lb (12,701 kg) of bombs (defensive) 13 0.5-in (12.7-mm) Browning machine-guns located in one four-gun barbette and three two-gun barbettes and in one three-gun tail turret

Powerplant: four 3,500-hp (2,611-kw) Pratt & Whitney R-4360-35A turbocharged radial piston engines

Performance:
maximum speed 380 mph (612 km/h) at 25,000 ft (7,620 m)
cruising speed 277 mph (445 km/h)
initial climb rate 2,165 ft (660 m) per minute
service ceiling 36,700 ft (11,185 m)
range 4,900 miles (7,885 km)

Weights:
empty equipped 80,609 lb (36,564 kg)
normal take-off —
maximum take-off 173,000 lb (78,473 kg)

Dimensions:
span as for B-50A
length
height
wing area

WB-50D Superfortress

Type:	weather-reconnaissance aircraft
Accommodation:	10–12
Armament:	none
Powerplant:	as for B-50D

Performance:

maximum speed	405 mph (652 km/h) at 30,000 ft (9,145 m)
cruising speed	272 mph (438 km/h)
initial climb rate	—
service ceiling	43,000 ft (13,105 m)
range	11 hours 30 minutes (endurance)

Weights:

empty equipped	—
normal take-off	—
maximum take-off	164,500 lb (74,617 kg)

Dimensions:

span	as for B-50D
length	
height	
wing area	

TB-50H Superfortress

Type:	training aircraft
Accommodation:	8
Armament:	none
Powerplant:	four 3,500-hp (2,611-kw) Pratt & Whitney R-4360-51 turbo-charged radial piston engines

Performance:

maximum speed	418 mph (673 km/h) at 31,000 ft (9,450 m)
cruising speed	410 mph (660 km/h) at 35,000 ft (10,670 m)
initial climb rate	2,270 ft (692 m) per minute
service ceiling	35,000 ft (10,670 m)
range	5,000 miles (8,047 km)

Weights:

empty equipped	78,970 lb (35,821 kg)
normal take-off	—
maximum take-off	120,000 lb (54,432 kg)

Dimensions:

span	as for B-50D
length	
height	
wing area	

KB-50J Superfortress

Type:	inflight-refuelling tanker
Accommodation:	6
Armament:	none
Powerplant:	as for B-50D plus two 5,900-lb (2,676-kg) thrust General Electric J47-23 turbojets

Performance:

maximum speed	444 mph (715 km/h) at 17,000 ft (5,180 m)
cruising speed	367 mph (591 km/h)
initial climb rate	3,260 ft (994 m) per minute
service ceiling	39,700 ft (12,100 m)
range	2,300 miles (3,700 km)

Weights:

empty equipped	93,200 lb (42,276 kg)
normal take-off	—
maximum take-off	179,500 lb (81,421 kg)

Dimensions:

span	141 ft 3 in (43.05 m)
length	105 ft 1 in (32.03 m)
height	33 ft 7 in (10.24 m)
wing area	1,720 sq ft (159.79 m²)

Boeing Model 345 (B-29 Superfortress) technical description

Type: four-engine strategic bomber.
Wings: mid-wing monoplane of cantilever structure using 24ST aluminium alloy; wing section Boeing 117; 7° sweepback on the leading edge and straight trailing edge; 4½° dihedral; the wing was built in five sections, comprising a centre section running through the fuselage, two outer sections and two wingtip sections, using an all-metal web type of structure covered with a butt-jointed metal skin flush-riveted throughout; lateral control effected by statically and aerodynamically balanced ailerons with combination servo and trim tabs; electrically operated trailing-edge flaps moved back as well as down when operated to increase wing area by some 19 per cent.
Fuselage: circular-section semi-monocoque structure of aluminium alloy, built in five pieces and using circumferential bulkheads and frames with extruded longerons and stringers, covered with butt-joined and flush-riveted stressed metal skinning; two bomb bays, located fore and aft of the wing main carry-through structure; three pressurised compartments,

those in the nose and amidships connected by a crawlway over the bomb bays, but the rear turret isolated from the others.
Tail unit: cantilever monoplane structure with all-metal fixed surfaces and fabric-covered metal-framed control surfaces of statically and aerodynamically balanced type with controllable trim-tabs.
Landing gear: retractable tricycle type, the main units having twin wheels and two oleo-pneumatic shock struts, and the nose unit twin wheels and a single oleo-pneumatic shock strut; electric actuation, the main units retracting rearwards into the rear of the inboard engine nacelles, and the steerable nose unit rearwards into a well underneath the flightdeck; hydraulic brakes on all six wheels; retractable tail bumper under fixed portion of the tail-plane.
Powerplant and fuel system: four 2,200-hp (1,641-kw) Wright R-3350-57 Double Cyclone 18-cylinder air-cooled radial piston engines, each with a General Electric turbocharger located vertically on each side of its low-drag nacelle; four-blade Hamilton-Standard Hydromatic

constant-speed fully-feathering propellers, each having a diameter of 16 ft 7 in (5.05 m); one self-sealing oil tank in each nacelle, and 5,608 US gal (21,229 litres) of fuel in self-sealing integral wing cells.
Accommodation: provision for a flight crew of between 10 and 14, the normal crew consisting of a pilot, co-pilot, navigator, bombardier, flight engineer and radio operator (forward compartment) and four gunners (three in midships compartment and the fourth in the tail position); the pilot and co-pilot sat side-by-side in the upper nose, with the bombardier between and below them, the navigator facing forward behind the pilot, the engineer facing aft behind the co-pilot and the radio operator behind the engineer; all crew positions were protected by armour or Flak curtains; compartment pressurisation was effected by two superchargers driven by the inboard engines.
Armament: four General Electric electrically controlled and operated turrets, in fore and aft pairs above and below the fuselage, all on the centreline; the forward

55

dorsal turret contained four 0.5-in (12.7-mm) Colt-Browning M2 machine-guns, and the other three each contained two 0.5-in (12.7-mm) Colt-Browning M2 machine-guns; the Bell tail turret was electrically operated and contained one 20-mm M2 Type B cannon and two 0.5-in (12.7-mm) Colt-Browning M2 machine-guns, or alternatively two 0.5-in (12.7-mm) Colt-Browning M2 machine-guns; in the B-29B the tail position was fitted with three 0.5-in (12.7-mm) Colt-Browning M2 machine-guns, and there was provision for two manually operated 0.5-in (12.7-mm) Colt-Browning M2 machine-guns in the waist; the B-29B retained provision for the retrofitting of the standard turrets, but the weight saved by the removal of the turrets/sighting blisters permitted an extra 3,000 lb (1,361 kg) of bombs, while the reduced drag boosted maximum speed by 10 mph (16 km/h); maximum conventional bombload was 20,000 lb (9,072 kg), carried in twin bays with electrically operated doors.

Superfortress production

XB-29: three prototypes (41-002, 41-003 and 41-18335)
YB-14: 14 service-test aircraft (41-36954/41-36967)
B-29-BW: 1,634 aircraft built by Boeing Wichita (42-6205/42-6454, 42-24420/42-24919, 44-69655/ 44-70154, 44-87584/44-87783 and 45-21693/45-21872)
B-29-MO: 536 aircraft built by Martin at Omaha (42-65202/42-65313, 42-65315/42-65401, 44-27259/ 44-27358 and 44-86242/44-86473)
B-29-BA: 357 aircraft built by Bell at Marietta (42-63352/42-63751 including 168 completed as B-29Bs, and 44-83890/44-84156 including 143 completed as B-29Bs and four cancelled)
B-29A-BN: 1,119 built by Boeing Renton (42-93824/42-94123 and 44-61510/44-62328)
B-50A: 79 aircraft built by Boeing Seattle (46-002/46-060 and 47-098/ 47-117)
B-50B: 45 aircraft built by Boeing Seattle (47-118/47-162)
B-50D: 222 aircraft built by Boeing Seattle (47-163/47-170, 48-046/ 48-127 and 49-260/49-391)
TB-50H: 24 aircraft built by Boeing Seattle (51-447/51-470)

Acknowledgments

We would particularly like to thank Mr Gordon S. Williams of the Boeing Commercial Airplane Company and Ms Marilyn Phipps of Boeing Historical Services for their invaluable help with the pictures for this publication.

Picture research was through Military Archive & Research Services and unless otherwise indicated below all material was supplied by Boeing.

Jeremy Flack/Aviation Photographers International: pp. 26 (top left, top right, bottom), 27.
Stuart Howe: pp. 4–5, 21, 24 (top right, 25 (inset), 26 (centre).
Imperial War Museum: p. 35.
Kerr/Aviation Photographers International: p. 51 (bottom).
US Air Force: pp. 13, 32, 33, 36–37, 43.